THE LITTLE BOOK OF
WISDOM

Parts of this book were first published in 2020 by Trigger, an imprint of Shaw Callaghan Ltd.

This expanded edition published in 2023 by OH! an Imprint of Welbeck Non-Fiction Limited, part of Welbeck Publishing Group. Offices in: London – 20 Mortimer Street, London W1T 3JW and Sydney – 205 Commonwealth Street, Surry Hills 2010 www.welbeckpublishing.com

Disclaimer:

OH! encourages diversity and different viewpoints. However, all views, thoughts, and opinions expressed in this book are not necessarily representative of Welbeck Publishing Group as an organization. All material in this book is set out in good faith for general guidance; no liability can be accepted for loss or expense incurred in following the information given. In particular, this book is not intended to replace expert medical or phychiatric advice. It is intended for informational purposes only and for your own personal use and guidance. It is not intended to diagnose, treat or act as a substitute for professional medical advice.

ISBN 978-1-80069-358-6

Editorial: Victoria Denne
Project manager: Russell Porter
Production: Jess Brisley

A CIP catalogue record for this book is available from the British Library

Printed in China

10 9 8 7 6 5 4 3 2 1

THE LITTLE BOOK OF
WISDOM

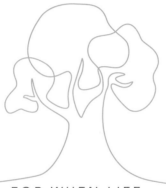

FOR WHEN LIFE
GETS A LITTLE TOUGH

CONTENTS

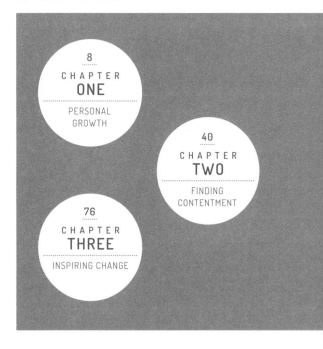

INTRODUCTION

We often think of wisdom as something reserved only for the elderly or educated and gained through life experience, however wisdom has a depth and nuance that can be fostered by considering perspective in relation to knowledge. This age-old saying sums it up well: "Knowledge is knowing what to say. Wisdom is knowing when to say it."

The Little Book of Wisdom offers guidance from some of the world's greatest minds in the art of making wise decisions that keep your immediate needs in mind, while maintain long-term perspective. As you'll soon discover, a little wisdom can go a long way in supporting choices you make in all aspects of your life.

CHAPTER

1

PERSONAL GROWTH

Reframe your own narrative,
cultivate meaningful changes, and
strive to be a better version of
yourself every day.

Be as you wish to seem.

Socrates

Yesterday is history, tomorrow is a mystery, today is God's gift, that's why we call it the present.

Anonymous

Those who improve with age embrace
the power of personal growth and
personal achievement and begin to
replace youth with wisdom, innocence

with understanding, and lack of
purpose with self-actualization.

Bo Bennett

I have just three things to teach:
simplicity, patience, compassion. These
three are your greatest treasures.

Lao Tzu

Grief can be the garden of compassion. If you keep your heart open through everything, your pain can become your greatest ally in your life's search for love and wisdom.

Rumi

We are what our thoughts have made us; so take care about what you think. Words are secondary. Thoughts live; they travel far.

Swami Vivekananda

Being entirely honest with
oneself is a good exercise.

Sigmund Freud

A wise man is superior to any insults which can be put upon him, and the best reply to unseemly behaviour is patience and moderation.

Moliére

By three methods we may learn
wisdom: First, by reflection, which
is noblest; Second, by imitation, which
is easiest; and third by experience,
which is the bitterest.

Confucius

There are many ways of going forward,
but only one way of standing still.

Franklin D. Roosevelt

If you set out to be liked, you would be prepared to compromise on anything at any time, and you would achieve nothing.

Margaret Thatcher

To enjoy good health, to bring
true happiness to one's family,
to bring peace to all, one must
first discipline and control one's
own mind. If a man can control his

mind he can find the way
to Enlightenment, and all of
wisdom and virtue will naturally
come to him.

Buddha

Patience is the companion of wisdom.

Saint Augustine

Teach your children poetry; it opens the mind, lends grace to wisdom and makes the heroic virtues hereditary.

Walter Scott

Count your age by friends, not years.
Count your life by smiles, not tears.

John Lennon

One's philosophy is not best expressed
in words; it is expressed in the choices
one makes and the choices we make are
ultimately our responsibility.

Eleanor Roosevelt

In dwelling, live close to the ground.
In thinking, keep to the simple.
In conflict, be fair and generous.
In governing, don't try to control.

In work, do what you enjoy.
In family life, be completely present.

Lao Tzu

Habit, if not resisted, soon becomes necessity.

Saint Augustine

Through perseverance many
people win success out of
what seemed destined to
be certain failure.

Benjamin Disraeli

It does not matter how slowly you go,
as long as you do not stop.

Confucius

We must become the change
we want to see.

Mahatma Gandhi

Life isn't about finding yourself.
Life is about creating yourself.

George Bernard Shaw

God grant me the serenity to accept the things I cannot change, courage to change the things I can, and wisdom to know the difference.

Reinhold H. Niebuhr

Be like water making its way through cracks. Do not be assertive, but adjust to the object, and you shall find a way round or through it. If nothing within you stays rigid, outward things will disclose themselves.

Bruce Lee

I will speak ill of no one and speak
all the good I know of everybody.

Andrew Jackson

People often say that motivation
doesn't last. Well, neither does bathing ...
that's why we recommend it daily.

Zig Ziglar

CHAPTER

2

FINDING CONTENTMENT

Achieving a state of peaceful
happiness in all aspects of life
allows us to appreciate what we
have in the here and now.

My advice to you is not to inquire why or whither, but just enjoy your ice cream while it's on your plate.

Thornton Wilder

True wisdom comes to each of us when
we realize how little we understand about
life, ourselves, and the world around us.

Socrates

I don't have everything I want but I have everything I need. That's contentment.

James MacDonald

Make it your habit not to be critical about small things.

Edward Everett Hale

When life gets you down do you
wanna know what you've gotta do?
Just keep swimming.

Dory, *Finding Nemo*

With pride, there are many curses. With humility, there come many blessings.

Ezra Taft Benson

At some point, you gotta let go,
and sit still, and allow contentment
to come to you.

Elizabeth Gilbert

In wisdom gathered over time,
I have found that every experience
is a form of exploration.

Ansel Adams

It's almost impossible to be satisfied in your own life if you're constantly looking at what someone else has.

Rachael Cruze

Experience is not what happens
to you; it's what you do with
what happens to you.

Aldous Huxley

Now and then it's good to pause in our pursuit of happiness and just be happy.

Henry Fielding

All things must come to the soul from
its roots, from where it is planted.

Saint Teresa of Avita

A harvest of peace is produced
from a seed of contentment.

Proverb

To know how to grow old is the master work of wisdom, and one of the most difficult chapters in the great art of living.

Herman Melville

Don't gain the world and lose your soul;
wisdom is better than silver or gold.

Bob Marley

The only true wisdom is in knowing you know nothing.

Socrates

Always keep your mind as bright
and clear as the vast sky, the
great ocean, and the highest peak,
empty of all thoughts. Always keep

your body filled with light and heat.
Fill yourself with the power of
wisdom and enlightenment.

Morihei Ueshiba

We humans have lost the wisdom
of genuinely resting and relaxing.
We worry too much. We don't allow
our bodies to heal, and we don't allow
our minds and hearts to heal.

Thich Nhat Hanh

Everything comes to us that belongs to us
if we create the capacity to receive it.

Rabindranath Tagore

Sometimes I am happy and
sometimes not. I am, after all,
a human being, you know. And I
am glad that we are sometimes

happy and sometimes not. You get your wisdom working by having different emotions.

Yoko Ono

Blessed are those who give
without remembering and
take without forgetting.

Elizabeth Bibesco

True contentment is not having
everything, but in being satisfied
with everything you have.

Oscar Wilde

Be content with what you
have; rejoice in the way things
are. When you realize there
is nothing lacking, the whole
world belongs to you.

Lao Tzu

I have learned to seek my happiness by limiting my desires, rather than in attempting to satisfy them.

John Stuart Mill

There is a difference between
happiness and wisdom: he that
thinks himself the happiest man
is really so but he that thinks

himself the wisest is generally
the greatest fool.

Francis Bacon

A grateful person is rich in contentment.

David Bednar

Self-esteem is crucial to how
much or how little contentment
you feel at the end of your life.

Mark Goulston

. True contentment is a thing as active as agriculture. It is the power of getting out of any situation all that there is in it. It is arduous and it is rare.

Gilbert K. Chesterton

Life is not a problem to be solved but a
reality to be experienced.

Søren Kierkegaard

Be thankful for what you have;
you'll end up having more. If you
concentrate on what you don't have,
you will never, ever have enough.

Oprah Winfrey

It isn't what you have or who you are
or where you are or what you are
doing that makes you happy or unhappy.
It is what you think about it.

Dale Carnegie, *How to Win Friends and Influence People*

CHAPTER
3

INSPIRING CHANGE

Awaken your mind to new
possibilities by breaking down the
barriers of your own expectations
and perceived limitations.

Things don't have to change
the world to be important.

Steve Jobs

Without freedom of thought, there can be no such thing as wisdom – and no such thing as public liberty without freedom of speech.

Benjamin Franklin

Never tell people how to do things.
Tell them what to do and they will
surprise you with their ingenuity.

George S. Patton

Everyone thinks of changing the world,
but no one thinks of changing himself.

Leo Tolstoy

And I love that even in the toughest moments, when we're all sweating it – when we're worried that the bill won't pass and it seems like all is lost – Barack never lets himself get distracted by the chatter and the noise. Just like his grandmother, he just keeps getting up and moving forward with patience and wisdom, and courage and grace.

Michelle Obama

To make no mistakes is not in the power of man; but from their errors and mistakes the wise and good learn wisdom for the future.

Plutarch

If you have the guts to keep making mistakes, your wisdom and intelligence leap forward with huge momentum.

Holly Near

The measure of intelligence
is the ability to change.

Albert Einstein

A good head and a good heart are always a formidable combination.

Nelson Mandela

Both old and young alike ought to seek wisdom: the former in order that, as age comes over him, he may be young in good things because of the grace of what has been, and the latter in order that, while he is young he may at the same time be old, because he has no fear of the things which are to come.

Epicurus

How wonderful is it that nobody
need wait a single moment before
starting to improve the world.

Anne Frank

Never interrupt someone doing what
you said couldn't be done.

Amelia Earhart

The price of doing the same old thing is far higher than the price of change.

Bill Clinton

Change will not come if we wait for some other person or some other time. We are the ones we've been waiting for. We are the change that we seek.

Barack Obama

Leave no stone unturned.

Euripides

Education is the most powerful weapon
which you can use to change the world.

Nelson Mandela

We gain the strength of the temptation we resist.

Ralph Waldo Emerson

Every great dream begins with a dreamer.
Always remember, you have within you
the strength, the patience, and the passion
to reach for the stars to change the world.

Harriet Tubman

It is better to risk starving to
death than surrender. If you give
up on your dreams, what's left?

Jim Carrey

A little knowledge that acts is worth infinitely more than much knowledge that is idle.

Khalil Gibran

Cynicism masquerades as wisdom,
but it is the furthest thing from it.
Because cynics don't learn anything.
Because cynicism is a self-imposed
blindness: a rejection of the world
because we are afraid it will hurt us

or disappoint us. Cynics always say 'no.' But saying 'yes' begins things. Saying 'yes' is how things grow.

Stephen Colbert

Knowledge without justice ought to be called cunning rather than wisdom.

Plato

Do, or do not. There is no try.

Yoda

CHAPTER
4

POSITIVE RELATIONSHIPS

Build and maintain healthy relationships with friends and loved ones to support your own happiness and wellbeing.

A tree is known by its fruit; a man by his deeds. A good deed is never lost; he who sows courtesy reaps friendship, and he who plants kindness gathers love.

Saint Basil

It is the neglect of timely repair that
makes rebuilding necessary.

Richard Whately

We can improve our relationships
with others by leaps and bounds if we
become encouragers instead of critics.

Joyce Meyer

My father said there were two kinds
of people in the world: givers and
takers. The takers may eat better,
but the givers sleep better.

Marlo Thomas

Too often we underestimate the power of a touch, a smile, a kind word, a listening ear, an honest compliment or the smallest act

of caring, all of which have the
potential to turn a life around.

Leo Buscaglia

The purpose of a relationship is not to have another who might complete you, but to have another with whom you might share your completeness.

Neale Donald Walsch

To know one's self is wisdom,
but not to know one's
neighbours is genius.

Minna Antrim

Being a mother is an attitude, not a biological relation.

Robert A. Heinlein, *Have Space Suit—Will Travel*

#1 relationship rule:
over communicate

Carlos Del Valle

Kindness is more important than
wisdom, and the recognition of this
is the beginning of wisdom.

Theodore Isaac Rubin

Sometimes two people have to
fall apart to realize how much they
need to fall back together.

Anonymous

That old law about 'an eye for an eye' leaves everybody blind. The time is always right to do the right thing.

Martin Luther King, Jr

Successful relationships start by giving up control, giving up the need to be loved or wanted or right all the time.

Mark Manson

Just as treasures are uncovered from the earth, so virtue appears from good deeds, and wisdom appears from a pure and peaceful mind. To walk safely through the

maze of human life, one needs
the light of wisdom and the
guidance of virtue.

Buddha

To know when to go away and when to come closer is the key to any lasting relationship.

Doménico Cieri Estrada

We all grow up. Hopefully, we get wiser. Age brings wisdom, and fatherhood changes one's life completely.

Frank Abagnale

Don't taunt the alligator until
after you've crossed the creek.

Dan Rather

We cannot control a relationship.
We can only contribute to a relationship.
All relationships, business or personal,
are an opportunity to serve another
human being.

Simon Sinek

Every man is a damn fool for at
least five minutes every day; wisdom
consists in not exceeding the limit.

Elbert Hubbard

None knows the weight of
another's burden.

George Herbert

The most profound relationship we will
ever have is the one with ourselves.

Shirley MacLaine

The meeting of two personalities
is like the contact of two chemical
substances: if there is any reaction,
both are transformed.

Carl Jung

The opportunity for brotherhood
presents itself every time you meet
a human being.

Jane Wyman

Everything that irritates us
about others can lead us to an
understanding of ourselves.

Carl Jung

CHAPTER

5

ACHIEVING SUCCESS

Setting personal goals can ensure you live each day with intention and harness the motivation to succeed.

Success is not final;
failure is not fatal:
It is the courage to
continue that counts.

Winston S. Churchill

Wise men make more
opportunities than they find.

Francis Bacon

Knowledge comes, but wisdom
lingers. It may not be difficult to
store up in the mind a vast quantity
of facts within a comparatively
short time, but the ability to form

judgements requires the severe
discipline of hard work and
the tempering heat of
experience and maturity.

Calvin Coolidge

When it is obvious that the goals cannot be reached, don't adjust the goals, adjust the action steps.

Confucius

Every day the clock resets.
Your wins don't matter.
Your failures don't matter.
Don't stress on what was,
fight for what could be.

Sean Higgins

Success usually comes to those who
are too busy to be looking for it.

Henry David Thoreau

Stop chasing the money and
start chasing the passion.

Tony Hsieh

Try not to become a person
of success, but rather try to
become a person of value.

Albert Einstein

Great minds discuss ideas;
average minds discuss events;
small minds discuss people.

Eleanor Roosevelt

Wisdom is the right use of knowledge. To know is not to be wise. Many men know a great deal, and are all the greater fools for it. There is no fool so great a

fool as a knowing fool.
But to know how to use
knowledge is to have wisdom.

Charles Spurgeon

I have not failed. I've just found
10,000 ways that won't work.

Thomas Edison

We should not judge people by
their peak of excellence, but by
the distance they have travelled from
the point where they started.

Henry Ward Beecher

Never let your head hang down.
Never give up and sit down and
grieve. Find another way. And don't
pray when it rains if you don't
pray when the sun shines.

Richard M. Nixon

The greater danger for most of us
lies not in setting our aim too high
and falling short; but in setting our aim
too low, and achieving our mark.

Michelangelo

We learn wisdom from failure much more than from success. We often discover what will do, by finding out what will not do and probably he

who never made a mistake never
made a discovery.

Samuel Smiles

You'll never do a whole lot
unless you're brave enough to try.

Dolly Parton

Don't be afraid to give up the
good to go for the great.

John D. Rockefeller

Success is the sum of small efforts,
repeated day-in and day-out.

Robert Collier

There are two types of people who will tell you that you cannot make a difference in this world: those who are afraid to try and those who are afraid you will succeed.

Ray Goforth

I find that the harder I work,
the more luck I seem to have.

Thomas Jefferson

All progress takes place outside
the comfort zone.

Michael John Bobak

A mistake is simply another
way of doing things.

Katharine Graham

Learning sleeps and snores in libraries, but wisdom is everywhere, wide awake, on tiptoe.

Josh Billings

If you're trying to achieve, there will be roadblocks. I've had them; everybody has had them. But obstacles don't have to stop you. If you run into a wall don't turn

around and give up. Figure out
how to climb it, go through it,
or work around it.

Michael Jordan

Back of every mistaken venture
and defeat is the laughter of
wisdom, if you listen.

Carl Sandburg

I am the master of my fate;
I am the captain of my soul.

William Ernest Henley

CHAPTER

6

THOUGHTFUL REFLECTION

Reflecting on our lives and the
world around us allows us to
deepen our understanding
of who we are and transform
our perspective on the
challenges we face.

I'd rather regret the things
I've done than regret the things
I haven't done.

Lucille Ball

Knowledge is knowing
that a tomato is a fruit.
Wisdom is knowing not
to put it in a fruit salad.

Brian O'Driscoll

Swim upstream. Go the other way.
Ignore the conventional wisdom.

Sam Walton

The doorstep to the temple
of wisdom is a knowledge
of our own ignorance.

Benjamin Franklin

People don't notice whether it's winter or summer when they're happy.

Anton Chekhov

Only put off until tomorrow
what you are willing to die
having left undone.

Pablo Picasso

People spend too much time finding other people to blame, too much energy finding excuses for not being what they are capable of being, and not enough energy

putting themselves on the line,
growing out of the past, and
getting on with their lives.

Michael Straczynski

What would life be if we had
no courage to attempt anything?

Vincent Van Gogh

The more you are like yourself,
the less you are like anyone else,
which makes you unique.

Walt Disney

To profit from good advice requires
more wisdom than to give it.

Wilson Mizner

Never interrupt your enemy
when he is making a mistake.

Napoleon Bonaparte

Wisdom begins in wonder.

Socrates

The philosophy of life is this: Life is not a struggle, not a tension. Life is bliss. It is eternal wisdom, eternal existence.

Maharishi Mahesh Yogi

Imagination is more important
than knowledge.

Albert Einstein

Our happiness depends
on wisdom all the way.

Sophocles

The man who makes everything that leads to happiness depend upon himself, and not upon other men, has adopted the very best plan for living happily. This is the man of moderation, the man of manly character and of wisdom.

Andrew Carnegie

The pessimist complains about the wind;
the optimist expects it to change...
the realist adjusts the sails.

William Arthur Ward

The wheel that squeaks the loudest
is the one that gets the grease.

Josh Billings

It's better to be a lion for a day
than a sheep all your life.

Elizabeth Kenny

The more sand that has escaped
from the hourglass of our life, the
clearer we should see through it.

Jean Paul

Look at anyone's bookcase
at home, no matter how modest,
and you're going to find a book that
contains wisdom or ideas
or a language that's at least a
thousand years old.

And the ideas that humans have created a mechanism to time travel, to hurl ideas into the future, it sort of bookends. Books are a time machine.

Jonathan Nolan

Do not go where the pay may lead, go instead where there is no path and leave a trail.

Ralph Waldo Emerson

Each of us finds his unique vehicle for sharing with others his bit of wisdom.

Ram Dass

Wisdom ceases to be wisdom
when it becomes too proud to weep,
too grave to laugh, and too selfish
to seek other than itself.

Khalil Gibran